NUTS ABOUT DATA

DATA

A STORY OF HOW DATA SCIENCE IS CHANGING OUR LIVES

MEOR AMER

NUTS ABOUT DATA

Copyright © 2019 by Meor Amer.

Heatmaps from RSAT. Maze from http://mazegenerator.net/.

For information contact :
contact@edsquarelabs.com

ISBN: 9789671727201

First Edition: Sep 2019

While the story is a work of fiction, the technical concepts explained throughout this book are real and practical.

Contents

Chapter 1: Begin 5

Chapter 2: Define 15

Chapter 3: Collect 25

Chapter 4: Analyze 38

Chapter 5: Explore 53

Chapter 6: Model 68

Chapter 7: Tune 84

Chapter 8: Redefine 95

Chapter 9: Storytell 105

Epilogue 120

About the Author 126

Chapter 1
Begin

THE DAWN OF a new day in Nutancia was the kind of breezy, radiant morning that would spur you on with hope and inspiration. However, Aly was short of both, just when he needed them desperately. For hours, he had been pacing back and forth in his small burrow. In sharp contrast to the glorious sunrise, he could only see gloomy days ahead. He couldn't stop thinking about the worst. *What am I going to do? We have nowhere to turn to. We're doomed*, he thought.

Nutancia was well-known for its resources of nuts. At the heart of this squirrel country, there was a deep square maze where nuts could be found every single day. It contained every variety:

walnuts, acorns, pecans, almonds, pistachios; the list goes on. The nature of the maze dictated that these nuts would emerge from the ground and make their way onto the surface.

One challenging part about it was that the place and time in which the nuts emerged were random. This was a big deal for such a deep maze with endless loops and dead ends. No matter how many hours you spent, if you were at the wrong times and places, you would come away with nothing.

Four squirrel clans lived in this country, each near a corner of the maze. The clans spent most of their time hunting for these nuts to feed their squirrels. Each corner of the maze had an entry. Every day, hordes of "nut miners" as they were called, would go into the maze via these entries, scour for the nuts, and return with their collections.

The maze was an unforgiving place where the clans competed fiercely to beat each other to the nuts they so desired. Three of these clans, Groar, Globb, and Grint were known for their large populations and strength. They prepared their miners well through sophisticated training regimes. Because of this, they were involved in a perennial competition to outnumber, outmuscle, and outthink each other, setting higher standards all the time.

Meanwhile, the other clan, Gliff, was smaller in number. The methods they used to train their miners were nowhere near as good as those of the other three, and because of that, the desire to compete was not on their agenda. As long as they managed to scrape together enough nuts to live adequately, they were happy.

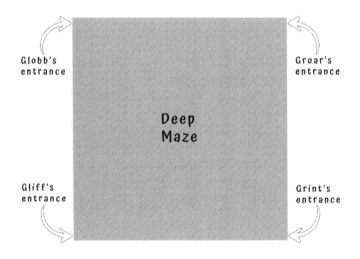

Sometimes, droughts happened, and that's when they really struggled. Thankfully, the droughts never lasted too long, and every time, they would manage to build just enough reserves of nuts to keep them going. Given a choice, they would jump at the chance of having a more comfortable life. But they weren't complaining.

Things, however, took a turn in the past year. The drought was nothing like what they had seen before. Nuts had become much harder to come by, and as a result, their reserves steadily declined. With no sign of this improving, for the first time in their lives, they were staring at the possibility of prolonged starvation.

Gone were the days when the Gliff town was buzzing as squirrels met and enjoyed each other's company. The younger ones were told to stay at home instead of exploring life out in the woods. Conserving energy in the face of scarcity was one thing, but, more than that, the misery of facing a bleak future was dampening their spirits. Their joy and optimism were slowly going away.

Their lives were now all about struggle, grinding by each day with barely enough nuts to eat. Most of the time, they would have to ration the food supply among themselves and stay hungry for days, sometimes even weeks.

Going into the maze became an even more

arduous task for the miners. They were feeding off scraps and would be lucky if they returned with something. They knew it's time they changed their ways, or otherwise, they would be facing extinction.

The onus was on Aly, the leader of Gliff, to come up with something. As he finally sat down on his chair, he thought, *This is nothing like what we've seen before. What makes me think there's a way out?!*

Aly came up through the ranks pouring his blood, sweat, and tears for the sake of the clan. He had been a loyal general to the clan's previous leader and gave everything he had to offer. No leader was more genuine and cared more deeply about his clan than Aly.

He had done it all. In fact, he had been a nut miner himself many years ago. That time was still one of the highlights of his life. He relished both the thrill of exploring the maze and the fulfillment of returning home with food to feed the squirrels. He knew the ins and outs of the mining operations and couldn't help from taking a hands-on approach even to this day, even when he had Lex, whom he entrusted to lead the mining team.

But even he had no idea of how to turn such

a colossal problem around. Uncharacteristically, he had finally let the pressure get the better of him. Most of the squirrels in his circle had, by now, gotten the bitter taste of his mood. Aly was in shambles and couldn't get his act together.

But he knew he needed to. *The other clans are getting stronger than ever*, he thought. *If I can't find a solution, Gliff will live on borrowed time. It's now or never.*

He needed to come up with a plan. *Maybe I should talk to Moe and see if he has anything interesting to say.*

Being a true leader, Aly had consulted with most, if not all, of the squirrels in his clan. Moe would probably be one of the last.

Moe was one rather curious character. He chose not to become one of the miners, unlike most of the squirrels of his age. Because of this, he wasn't well received within the clan. They accused him of being selfish and a slacker.

But Aly, like the rest of the clan, also knew that Moe was different from most in the way he saw things that others didn't. He had come up with inventions that were totally unheard of. Once, he showed a strange thing called a communication device that could be used by squirrels to talk to each other. Another time, he was showing a box with a screen showing texts and images. It's just that they didn't see the point.

Aly tended to agree that Moe should be spending his energy and time helping the clan find food, not pursuing futile endeavors. But right now, Aly just didn't care. *Nothing to lose. I'll pay him a visit tomorrow.*

✳ ✳ ✳

"So, what brings you here? I don't think we've spoken much before, have we?" Moe asked as Aly made his way into his burrow.

"Moe, you know our situation. It's not getting any better, and I need any help I can get. We've been pulling our fur out trying to figure out what else can be done, but we're nowhere near any solution."

"What makes you think I can help?"

"I know the squirrels haven't been too kind to you," Aly said. "But you don't know this part. They all told me the same thing about you. They said that you're forward-looking and never short of ideas."

"What do you expect from me, actually?"

I could do with a miracle. "No expectations. I just thought it's time I met smart squirrels like you, get your thoughts, and who knows, maybe we can find a way to turn this around."

Moe didn't seem to be interested at all. "I really don't know how I can help. Sorry to disappoint you."

Aly moved within inches from Moe and stared him down. "Listen, Moe. This is now about life and death. As much as I hate to say that, it's the reality. Even if you don't care, it will hit you soon enough!"

"Don't get me wrong," Moe said. "I just don't know how to help. Everything that I've been working on was just a hobby. That's it, nothing more than that. I don't know how they can be useful to you."

How can you be so detached from reality?! "I'm sure you can do better than that. Don't tell me there's nothing you can do with your inventions. What about those tiny little devices, or the funny-looking boxes, or the nut scanners—"

Moe jerked his head back. "Wait. Nut scanners!"

"What about them?"

"That just gave me an idea," Moe said, his eyes sparkling.

"Then tell me about it," Aly demanded.

But Moe became subdued almost as quickly. "But, on second thought, I don't know if it'll work. I'll probably just waste your time. It's just a theory and I've never really done it for real, let alone for this scale of a problem."

"Moe, let me be clear," Aly said, raising his voice. "I don't know why I'm putting so much trust in you. But I don't care because our clan is now in deep trouble. I'll take whatever chance I have. Now, I just have one question for you. Do you believe in that idea?"

"Um, I think so."

"Good enough for me. I'll take it. Now let's start."

"Start doing what?"

"Turning that idea into a plan."

Moe's face turned pale. "I don't have good feelings about this one. I don't know where to start, really. But if you insist, can I ask for a couple of things?"

"Fair enough. What are they?"

"First, I want you to promise to have patience," Moe said. "I know time is not on our side. But there are steps to be taken in anything that we do, even more so for this plan. If we rush through things, I'm afraid we'll end up going nowhere."

"You know I'm not a patient squirrel. But sure, I hear you loud and clear. What's the other request?"

"I need another squirrel to join us and work on this plan. And I think I know who that would be."

Chapter 2
Define

VERY FEW TALL, burly squirrels lived in Nutancia and Maq was one of them. He towered over most miners with his bulging muscles and presented a domineering figure, especially when he was mad. As Maq carefully scanned Groar's nut mining operations center, he couldn't help but feel proud of what he had created. *Poetry in motion*, he thought. From the unloading of newly collected nuts, sorting them into separate sections, and right until readying them for distribution, the whole process was a display of efficiency.

But this isn't enough. Maq didn't need reminding that times had changed. The maze's old rules wouldn't hold for much longer. He knew his miners would have their work cut out for them just to be able to maintain the same level of collection that they'd been amassing. Other clans looked to Groar as the standard in nut mining, but he wasn't stupid to think that they could afford to rest on their laurels. *We need to up our game.*

Being the leader of Groar for many years taught him that nothing could be taken for granted when it came to nut mining. He didn't need a reminder that like his predecessors, only one reason would continue to keep him at the helm: food.

He knew about the struggles of Gliff and, to a lesser degree, the other two clans. But why should he waste his time worrying about what troubles they were facing? *Why don't they just work harder? Success doesn't come free.*

He had only one goal. To keep his clan happy with his leadership by giving them the nuts they so craved. The more for Groar, the better.

∗ ∗ ∗

Back in Moe's burrow, Aly slumped into a

chair that Moe had offered him, his paws dropping to his sides. *What have I just got myself into?* Never in his life had he made such a rash decision. In one of the most pivotal moments in Gliff's history, let alone his life, he was banking on a clueless squirrel to turn an idea he had just thought of into a plan. *He hasn't even told me what the plan is!*

Moe had also asked him for some time before they could see any results. *Two weeks! At least?! That's an eternity.*

Moe appeared to hesitate before finally uttering, "Um, before I talk about my plan, do you mind if I first ask a few questions...?" He paused. "Actually, lots of them."

"You don't have to be so polite. Go ahead."

"Thanks, appreciate it," Moe said sheepishly. "First, can you tell me, at the end of each day, what do the miners report to their leaders?"

"The most obvious thing is, of course, the nuts themselves," Aly said. "Each miner will pass the collection for the day to the leaders. Since we need to keep track of our reserve, for each miner, we weigh the nuts that they've collected."

He looked across the table at Moe, who was jotting notes studiously in his notebook. He didn't have a clue of what to expect but decided to trust Moe, at least for now. "And, as we want to keep the miners accountable every day, we also record the date. We keep these records in a simple table that we add to daily."

Name	Date	Amount (grams)
Ben	25-Jan	350
Nat	25-Jan	146
Rob	25-Jan	242
Wim	25-Jan	78
...	...	...
...	...	...
...	...	...

"Okay, got it," Moe said. "What about the mining itself? Can you tell me how the miners go about doing their work?"

"We have around one hundred miners in total," Aly said. "Each of the other clans has almost double that number, so we have to be a bit more clever. We know that the maze is square, so we assign the miners according to zones in the maze."

"How many zones are there?"

"Nine."

"And how do you decide which squirrels go to

which zones?" Moe asked further.

Aly crossed his arms. "It's based on experience. The miners would have different zones that they know best, so those are where they will be deployed. But even within their own zones, the maze is just too vast for them to cover. In fact, no single clan can cover the whole maze at one time, no matter how many miners they send."

"What do you do about it then?"

"We just do our best, going to different parts of the maze each day. We also send less miners near the entrances of the other clans. They're just too many and too fast, so they'd collect all the nuts by the time we got there."

"Do you have a map of the maze?" Moe asked.

I saw that coming. "We don't," Aly said. "Our miners are the most dedicated and hardworking bunch I know. They've traveled to each and every corner of their zones, so the map is already there in their heads. They've never needed a map!"

"I trust that you know best," Moe said. "But don't you think having a map might be helpful?"

Aly drew a big sigh. "Of course we do. We just don't know how much, though. It's just one of those things that we've thought about and felt that it might be of some use, but just never had the time to do it. You know, every second of our miners' time is valuable."

"Is the maze open all the time?" Moe asked.

This kid has really been living in his own bubble, Aly thought. *Is this all going to be worth it?!*

"Yes, twenty-four seven," Aly said. "The miners work in shifts and we're there all the time. However, we've learned that there aren't as many nuts in the maze at night compared to daytime. That's why we don't send as many miners during the night, and we know the other clans are doing the same."

"Of course," Aly continued, "it's also a tougher place at night, being pitch dark, and our miners getting banged into by the other clans all the time. We've had plenty of injury cases due to that." He stood up and peered through the window as he thought about the dangers facing the miners every single day.

"Okay," Moe said, "let's now talk about the fun part: the nuts."

Aly sensed an air of confidence slowly seeping through Moe. "What about them?"

"When you gather all these nuts, do you take

note of their types?"

"That's a strange question. Why would we?"

Moe shrugged his shoulders. "I'm just asking if it's something you've considered."

Aly started to become annoyed at what he saw as a sign of flippancy bordering on disrespect from Moe. "You should know. The most important thing for us is to get enough supply of nuts to feed us all. That's it. We just don't have the luxury of choosing the nicer tasting types over the other. We just eat what we've got!" He shook his head, still smarting from that question.

"No, that's not where I'm coming from," Moe said. "I mean, could there be certain types of nuts that make us full longer than the others?"

"Oh, okay," Aly said, realizing he was being a bit harsh. "Maybe there are. I've heard a few squirrels saying that, and probably you have as well. But even if it were true, the difference wouldn't be obvious. We wouldn't be able to tell for sure."

"What about the time it takes for them to go bad?" Moe asked. "Is there any difference between the types of nuts?"

Testing my patience again. "Listen, Moe," Aly

said. "We know nuts can last long. Maybe some, like almonds, last longer than the others, almost a year before they go bad. But for us Gliffs, it doesn't really matter. We would've eaten all of them by that time!"

"I think that's all for my questions. At least for now," Moe said.

"Good, because I was about to tell you to stop anyway. Now let's quickly get to the plan!"

"This *is* part of the plan," Moe said.

"What do you mean?"

"See," Moe said, "I may have an idea or even a solution. But if don't understand the problem clearly, I won't be able to make the idea useful. That's why I need experienced squirrels like you who have the *domain expertise* and truly understand the problem that we're solving."

"Okay, that's true," Aly said. "I can't disagree with that. But still, let's move quickly."

"I just wanted to mention one more thing," Moe said. "It's not exactly related to what we've discussed, but I've always had this in my mind."

"What is it?"

Moe was fidgeting for a moment and said, "What if the nuts in the maze were actually enough for all of us? I mean, all squirrels from all the clans put together. What if there were even way more than needed out there?"

Aly rolled his eyes. "Here's the thing, Moe. That's a noble thought and I wish we could all be in that place right now. But we won't. Never!"

"But, why not?" Moe didn't seem to be satisfied.

"See, the miners have been in the trenches, for years," Aly said. "It's a pipe dream, and I know this for a fact. If the nuts were so abundant, we wouldn't be here clutching at straws to come up with a half-decent plan." Aly started to regret dragging Moe into this mess. He felt as if he were getting further and further away from a solution. *The clock is ticking, and here I am listening to nonsense!*

Aly couldn't resist taking another swipe at Moe. "Let's even allow wishful thinking for a second and imagine if nuts were that easy to come by. Do you think the likes of Maq and his miners would be kind enough to step aside and let us have those nuts?!"

"Sorry if that offended you," Moe said. "I was just trying to think if a new truth were out there. But if it's not the case, then I accept. You know best."

"Okay then. What do we do next?"

"We'll focus on our most pressing problem: How can we get sufficient nuts supply to keep our clan nourished and healthy, despite all our limitations?"

"Very well summarized, I must say. Now tell me more."

"Aly, I know you won't like this, but it's been a long day," Moe said. "All this has been a whirlwind to me and I'm still struggling to put my thoughts together. Can you give me tonight to go through these again? Tomorrow, I'll talk to you about the plan."

Aly gave a disgruntled look. He had wished to get the answers that same day. But then, he recalled what Moe had told him earlier. *If we rush through things, we'll end up going nowhere.*

"Sure, we'll meet again, same time tomorrow," Aly said. *This better be good.*

"But can't you at least give me some idea of what your plan is going to be about?" Aly asked just before leaving.

"Sure. It's called data."

Chapter 3
Collect

MOE DRAGGED HIS footsteps as he approached his burrow's door to let Aly in, his paws shivering. He couldn't sleep last night, still coming to terms with what he had signed up for. He tossed and turned, thinking, *What if this failed? I'd be done with Gliff. I'd be exiled.*

He had somehow managed to stumble his way through the conversation with Aly yesterday. *Aly must have thought that I knew what I was doing.* He didn't.

But during those blurry moments, he held onto one thing he'd learned: *to understand the problem that you're solving, you need to ask all the right questions. But to get there, you'll inevitably be asking a lot of stupid questions.* He didn't know much about the mining operations, so he just followed his instinct and probed Aly with questions after questions, regardless of what Aly thought of them.

He had also pretended that he was on top of his plan when he asked for another squirrel to help. He wasn't. He knew that he couldn't come up with a plan all by himself, so he thought it was the right thing to do. But, contrary to what he had told Aly, he didn't know who that squirrel would be.

Throughout the night, he had managed to put together a rough concept of what the plan would look like. As he was reviewing it late into the night, the perfect candidate suddenly dawned on him.

"Please come in," Moe said to Aly. "If you don't mind, could we wait for Gil? She should be arriving anytime now. Have a seat."

As with most of the Gliff clan, Moe's burrow was simple and basic with nothing special inside, except for one corner where a few big boxes were lying around. Those were his "treasure chests," inside of which he had stuffed all the items he would use for his experiments. He didn't bother to tidy up, not even for the visit of his clan leader.

In the same corner stood a round table with a few chairs, where they were both now seated. A large white drawing board was within a couple of steps from the chairs; it was so huge that it almost covered the entire side of the wall.

Since arriving, Aly hadn't been looking too happy and the request to wait for Gil made him frown even more. "I know I agreed. But tell me, do we really need this? The more squirrels involved, the messier it will get. Things will get blown out of proportion."

"Aly, I'm not sure what the other squirrels had told you about me. But I'm no genius, and I can't work alone. I need help from others if we're going to make things happen."

Moe couldn't stop shifting in his chair as he quickly glanced out of the window, hoping to find Gil. "I had run this plan by her earlier this morning. I had also explained to her what I gathered from you yesterday. She's good at carrying out this step of the plan."

Moe was still shuddering at the thought of taking such a huge leap from a mere theory to solving a problem of this magnitude. But Gil agreeing to work on this plan and, now, her coming to the meeting had given him a much-needed boost of confidence. *This feels promising. Let's hope it turns out fine.*

"What step are you talking about?"

"There will be five distinct steps in our plan. We had gone through the first one yesterday when we defined the problem to solve. Now, the second step is called *data collection*. To take us through this step, we have Gil, our *data engineer*."

Aly looked puzzled. "What on earth is that?"

As Gil finally showed up at the front door, Moe said, "Don't worry, it's just a name. What's more important is what needs to be done. For this, I'll ask Gil to explain."

Moe didn't have many friends, but Gil was one of them. In fact, she was a long-time friend who shared Moe's passion for experimenting with new ideas. Within the clan, though, she was known for something else. They loved visiting her burrow because she was extremely good at space organization. She had all the different shelves arranged in the right corners. Each shelf would have its own theme of items, nicely grouped and perfectly balanced. The most impressive part was that she had organized all these into a well-structured design so she could instantly find any item whenever needed. Where others would end up with chaos, she had order.

"What I'm planning to do is to collect the data and organize them," Gil said. "From there, we can find patterns, reach conclusions, and plan our mining activities accordingly."

"Okay," Aly said, "there's a lot to unpack there. But what is this 'data' again?"

"Remember the nuts collection record that you've been keeping? That's data," Moe said. "Data is any information that you acquire and build over time. You've been using that data for the sole reason to keep track of how many nuts you collected and who collected them. But the same data can be used in many more ways."

"How else would you use the data?" Aly asked.

"For example, finding out where the nuts would most likely appear," Moe said. "That way, we can move our miners quickly to these locations, even faster than the other clans. It's about finding patterns and insights about the nuts."

Aly smirked. "That sounds good on paper. But how do we make it happen?"

"More work, of course! But it'll pay off," Moe said, signaling for Gil to take over.

Gil seemed unfazed by the challenge that they were facing. She appeared impressively comfortable with what she was dealing with and was completely focused on her task. "First, we need to draw the map of the maze—"

"I can't approve that," Aly interrupted. "That will mean the miners won't go to work. Drawing the map will require too much effort and time from the team."

Gil nodded. "I know, but we can plan so that there's little interruption to their jobs," she said. "We don't have to call them all at once. The miners have their own areas that they know best. We'll ask them to come one at a time and draw their portions."

"Okay then, that sounds more doable. We'll do it," Aly said, softening a little bit.

"I'll also need the miners to do a bit more while mining the nuts. They'll need to collect more data." Gil then took out her notebook and scribbled a word big enough for Aly and Moe to see. "Right now, each miner is already recording three types of information, or what we call *features:*

their names, the date of collection and the amount of nuts, in grams, collected for the day. Are you with me so far, Aly?"

"Yes, that seems straightforward. Three features."

"From now on, they'll need to collect more features."

Aly frowned. "I don't like the sound of this."

But Gil just smiled. "Just bear with me," she said. "We'll get to that, but let me first explain what those features are."

Gil went to the drawing board and started to write a list of items. "Every time they find a place with nuts, they must record the date, time, location, and the amount and type of nuts that they've collected."

She then added more items to the list. "They also need to collect a bunch of other features that tell us more about the environment where the nuts are found. For example, temperature, humidity, and brightness—"

"Stop! Now I'm definitely against this idea," Aly said, raising his voice. "There's no way they can do this, nor that they should. This means they'll move more slowly, having to do this every time. It'll hurt the collection!"

He was clearly unimpressed. He stood up from his chair and flapped his paw, dismissing the idea. "Besides, even if they wanted to, how on earth are they going to measure those features?"

"That's when they'll use this. Remember, it was *your* idea!" Moe grinned as he dug into a box next to him and brought out the nut scanner, a small, portable device with a pointed feature and a small glass surface at its front.

"Okay," Aly said, "to be honest, I've only heard about it from the other squirrels. But I don't really know what it does. Enlighten me."

"The scanner does precisely what Gil had just explained. I've designed it to collect all those features automatically."

"Just by pointing it at the nuts?"

"Yes." Moe's eyes gleamed with delight. "This is called technology."

"We can easily collect more features," Gil said, "but that's enough for now. We can always have more if required later."

Aly's jaw dropped, doing a poor job at concealing his admiration at what he was seeing. It felt like a turning point for Moe. *These years of hard work may not have been in vain after all*, he thought. It hadn't been easy for him with all the taunts and jibes from other squirrels. But rarely if ever did he let the opinions of others affect the belief he had in his work.

"I have to admit. This scanner is impressive. But... the whole plan is still vague to me," Aly said. "I still can't comprehend how this scanner and the data could actually solve our problems. Do I need to remind you that we don't have much time?"

"I know," Moe said. "That's why my very first request to you was patience. But, rest assured, you'll understand it once we've gone through all the steps. We'll speed it up as fast as we can, but it's still one step at a time. No shortcuts."

Did I just say that? The truth was, Moe was just trying to buy time. Yes, he had an overall concept in his mind. But the next level of details was still fuzzy to him. He knew he would need more than all his brainpower could ever muster. *I need more help. But first...the scanner.*

"The only thing I need help with now is to build more of these," he said. "If you can assign a few squirrels from our clan to help, we'll have enough in a couple of days."

Aly pressed his lips together, deliberating, then said, "Not a problem, if that's what it takes. I'll get ten squirrels to help you and whatever other resources you need..." He then paused, "But I'm still not convinced on one thing."

"What's that?"

"How can this scanner tell the type of the nut simply by scanning it? Don't you need a squirrel to do that?"

"I'll tell you the secret soon," Moe said. "I don't want to spend time on that now, it could take quite some time! By all means, bring this scanner home, test it out, and I think you'll be convinced."

"But since you asked, I think it's important that you understand *why* we need to know the type of nut in the first place," Gil added.

"Obviously," Aly said. "Otherwise, I wouldn't want to bother wasting my time testing the scanner."

"I asked Gil the same question I asked you," Moe said. "Do certain nuts make us full longer than the others? She did some research and found out that they do."

Gil reached out to her notebook and showed a list of all the different types of nuts and a "fullness" value for each. "The bigger the number means the longer it keeps us full. For example, pistachios can keep us full longer than most other nuts," she said. "In other words, if we collected the same amount of pistachios and almonds, we could last longer with the former."

"It's not a huge difference, but with our situation, every little bit counts," Moe added. "If our miners would now focus on finding pistachios first, then we could maximize our resources."

"I have to agree," Aly said. "With the small number of miners that we have, we need to think differently."

"And this is another nice thing about having data," Moe said. "We can create new features from existing features, called *feature engineering*. Combining the information from the amount of nuts collected and their fullness values, we'll have a better understanding of how long our reserve can actually last."

"One last thing, but an important one," Gil said. "Can I ask for a few more squirrels to help? This is for collecting and organizing the data. I'm sure you know about that box from Moe with a screen and some buttons."

"Yes, I've heard of it."

"It's called a computer. Now, this computer is important to us, as it'll process all the data and tell us many interesting things."

Gil took out her notebook again and drew two boxes. She wrote "Collect" in the first box and "Clean" in the second. "But before we can get to that stage, we need to do the less interesting tasks. We need to spend a lot of time looking at the data and cleaning it. The data is never perfect."

"But how do you *clean* data?" Aly asked.

"For example, the scanner may have stopped working for a while," Gil replied, "so it will have some missing data for that time. Or, it could be that some questionable information was reported, such as an unrecognizable location. In that case, we'll have to remove them and just keep the ones with valid information."

"The scanner isn't perfect and can malfunction sometimes," Moe added. "With the huge amount of data that we'll be collecting, the cleaning process will take a lot of time. That's why Gil is asking for some squirrels to help."

"Not a problem. I'll arrange for that. Now, let's get working. I need to see the outcome soon," Aly said.

"Great," Moe said. "Let's try this out and collect the data for a week."

Chapter 4
Analyze

MAQ DIDN'T LIKE what he was seeing. He had been in the mining arena for far too long to know that not even the slightest suspicion should be taken lightly.

Groar wasn't known to have the most accomplished of miners for no reason. For generations, the mining team had been equipped with not just the strength and endurance to win the mining battle but also the mental sharpness to be aware of their surroundings. They had been drilled to be alert at all times and to sense any unusual activities in the environment. Not a single observation would go unreported to the headquarters. Not even if it were coming from a clan as meek and harmless as Gliff.

What on earth are they up to? he thought as he was going through a report he'd just received from his miners. It mentioned that the miners from Gliff were carrying "strange little devices" and that "they were pointing these devices at the nuts they found."

Never would he associate this clan with any kind of ingenuity. *Not in a million years.* But just like how he had trained his miners, he knew this was something he shouldn't ignore. *Something fishy is going on here. Whatever it is, I can't let it continue.*

This kind of responsibility wasn't something Moe was accustomed to. In the past week, Lex, the head of the mining team, had confronted him several times, telling him to keep out of his territory. But Moe knew Lex had every reason to feel aggrieved. Even by their own standards, the nut mining team had never been put through such an ordeal. "They were the seven most grueling days of our lives," one of the miners had complained to Moe. As if they hadn't been stretched enough, they were now being asked to do even more.

First, they had to put the map together. The past week's nuts collection took a hit as the miners spent part of their time mapping out their areas with Gil. But she kept her word when she promised to Aly that interruption would be at a minimum. She had coordinated the whole process admirably, going step by step, area by area, and working with the miners one at a time.

Then, the nut scanner. The miners were already used to being super-focused, scurrying as swiftly as possible as they navigated the maze. A split-second delay meant that the other clans would beat them to the nuts. The scanning job meant that their momentum was lost.

The toughest part was yet to come. They were asked to cover more ground, way more than what they were used to. Moe had told them to scour deep into every single corner of the maze, including the vast areas they had usually avoided because they rarely found any nuts and areas too close to the other clans' entrances.

"I hope this will work, Gil," Moe said as they stood at his doorstep. "Otherwise, we'd better start packing up our bags and leave."

Aly arrived soon after, looking tense. Moe had heard from the miners about Aly's own run-ins with Lex about the raft of changes that he and Moe had introduced. His reputation as the clan's leader was on the line. News about this plan had slowly trickled down to the rest of the clan and expectations were building. *I know I need to repay his trust and deliver the goods,* Moe thought.

But as Aly entered Moe's burrow, his eyes bulged, seeing Bob, another squirrel from his clan, standing next to Gil and Moe. "Moe, what is he doing here?!"

"Sorry that I didn't inform you earlier," Moe said, "but the team needs more help. You don't know this, but Bob is perfect for the third step of the plan."

"Which is?" Aly said, still scowling.

"Bob is adept at performing *data analysis*," Moe said. "He's our *data analyst*. Today, we're going to do some analysis on the data that we've collected."

Bob was actually a popular squirrel among the clan. He had a charming personality and would always be seen mixing around among the clan. He also had a habit of always asking questions, with a particular fascination for what the squirrels do in their jobs. The nut miners were obvious targets, being a job so crucial to the livelihood of the clan.

Moe recalled some of Bob's conversations he'd listened to. *How many hours do you spend on this one task? Can you walk me through what you do for that task? Why are you doing it this way and not the other? Do you feel there's a better way to do it?* Bob could go on all day long.

"I guess all your time spent with the miners can now be put to good use," Aly said.

"I guess so," Bob said, smiling. "It was purely out of curiosity. I love to learn how squirrels do things. I guess I'm just obsessed about how we can do great work and how it can make us a better clan."

Bob's infectious passion could easily be felt, which meant Moe was spared from Aly's wrath this time. He knew that he was crossing the line, not asking for approval to bring Bob in.

"Okay now, let's get started," Moe said.

"Sure! First, let me present to you… the map of the maze," Bob said as he took a huge roll of paper and spread it on the floor. It was the first time they had seen such a complete map of the maze. It had all the details: the zones, passages, turns, dead ends, and everything you needed to know about it.

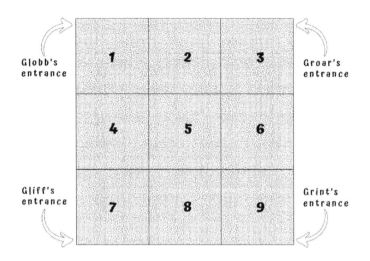

"I have to admit, this is a game-changer. Just being able to know the right paths to take or how far it takes to get to a certain place is invaluable," Aly said. His eyes gleamed as he looked at the map. It seemed as if his fury had subsided.

Thanks, Bob! Moe thought.

Aly continued, "I've always had to rely on each miner's experience for a specific area, but with this map, I can now assign any miner to any location."

"And we haven't even started talking about the data," Moe said.

"Okay, show me what you've got."

"We have the same map on the computer screen. Let's look at it," Bob said.

He then zoomed in on one of the zones, Zone 4, revealing the finer details of that part of the maze. "The more specific we get, the more precisely we know about the best places to find the nuts."

Map of the maze in Zone 4

"Hold on, are you saying that the computer can show where the nuts were?" Aly asked.

"Yes," Bob said. "That's coming from the data. Remember the different features that the scanners recorded? Those are where the data is coming from."

Bob then displayed on the screen a heatmap overlaid on top of the maze. "The computer made calculations on the data and used that to draw this heatmap. The darker the color, the more nuts there were."

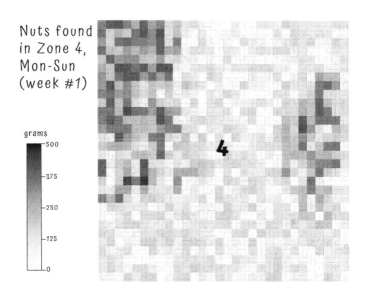

Nuts found in Zone 4, Mon-Sun (week #1)

grams
—500
—375
—250
—125
—0

"I must say, the data isn't perfect," Moe said. "It doesn't represent all the nuts in the maze, like those already nabbed by the other clans. But that's the point. We don't have to wait for perfection to get started. We can already gain a lot of—"

"Wait! This is strange," Aly interrupted, pointing to one particular spot on the screen. "The north-west of Zone 4. How could we find so many nuts there? No one in the right mind could've ever anticipated it."

Bob paused and then seemed to be trying to refresh the screen's view, pressing a key on the keyboard a few times. He looked puzzled as well. "This is strange indeed. It's so near to Globb's entrance. How could they have overlooked this?"

Moe had noticed the same thing, but his instinct told him that it was too good to be true. "But that will mean we have to ask them. Maybe next time!" he said, trying to steer away from the conversation. *Must be some bad data. Why didn't Gil detect them? Should've been cleaned already!* He didn't want Aly to catch him giving misleading information at such an early stage.

"But Aly's right," Bob said. "Something funny is going on there. We need to know what it is."

"I guess you're right," Moe said in a half-hearted tone. "What do you think we should do?"

Bob gave a long sigh. "To be honest, I don't know. Probably, we need to collect more data. Let's put this mysterious zone aside for now. We need time to think it through. But we must revisit it soon."

"The Mystery Zone. Intriguing…" Aly said.

"Never mind. What else do we need to do with this data?"

"We'll need to familiarize further with the data," Bob said.

Aly looked like he had question marks all over his face. "That's too vague. I don't understand."

"We can do this by asking questions and let the data answer them," Bob said. He smiled at seeing Aly's confused look. "I'll give one example. We may want to ask if these nuts only appeared at a certain day and time. If it turned out to be true, there would be no point for the miners to go there every day, all the time, right?"

Aly gave a crisp nod. "Okay, now I see where you're going. Makes sense."

Bob then changed the view on the screen from a map to a chart.

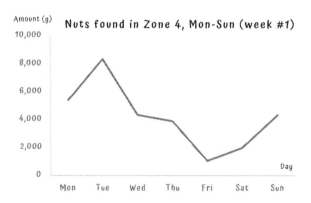

"Now, on the computer, I'm showing the nuts collected on the different days, from Monday to Sunday," he said.

"Interesting," Aly said, pointing to the chart. "It's clear that Tuesday had the biggest collection."

Bob then changed the chart to show the collections for Tuesday by the hour.

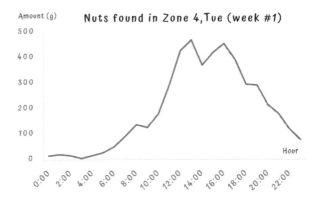

"I can even go further and show that on that day, peaks occurred between 1 and 5 p.m. when most of the nuts were found. Much fewer nuts were found during the other times," he said.

"And yet," Moe said, "we've only just scratched the surface."

***

Aly rubbed his chin as he tried to make sense of what he had seen so far. So many questions were running through his mind, but one, in particular, stood out. "We've looked at the data in the past week. From that, we now know where and when the most nuts *were* found."

Moe nodded.

"But then, how can you be sure that it will still be true next time?" Aly asked. "Are we sure that next week or, for that matter, months from now, Tuesdays will always give us more nuts? You know it doesn't work that way." He started to doubt Moe again as his mood swung from one extreme to the other.

"That's why I said we were just warming up!" Moe said with a wide grin. "But that's a great question and I was going to come to that. Now, let me explain."

Moe walked to the drawing board, took a pen and scrawled a couple of words. "Let's recall what we've done so far. We looked at the data and found some patterns. In other words, we understood 'what had happened'. This is called *descriptive analytics.*"

"Is it of any use then?" Aly asked.

"Of course, it is," Moe said. "It's extremely useful for us to summarize the data in a simple way, describe the highlights and identify the key observations."

"Such as the Mystery Zone," Bob added.

Moe swiftly turned to Bob and scowled at him, gesturing for him to cut it out. Aly didn't really understand what was going on, but one thing for sure, he was becoming increasingly restless. *Get quickly to the point!*

"But then, descriptive analytics won't truly answer 'why it happened'," Moe said. "We couldn't really make sense of what we saw, could we? Only by understanding the cause can we explain what really was going on there."

Moe went back to his chair and leaned closer to Aly as he stressed his next point. "Ultimately, it doesn't answer 'what will happen' in the future. Because of that, it's not enough to use that information to create a foolproof mining plan. We need something more."

"And what is that?" Aly asked.

"Something that can tell us about exactly that:

the future. And it turns out that it is possible."

"Seriously? How is that possible?" Aly didn't know if he should still hang around. All the information was just too much for him he couldn't tell if it were believable.

"Indeed, it's possible," Moe said. "And we can get the computer to do that."

He went back to the drawing board and wrote another word. "Okay, to put it more precisely, the computer can *predict* the future. We can train the computer and it will learn to the point it becomes very good at doing it."

"Wait a minute. This is making me dizzy. Train? Learn?"

"Yeah."

"Does the computer have a brain or something?" Aly resorted to sarcasm to vent his frustration. *This is bordering on insanity.*

"Well, something like that," Moe said. "We're going to train the computer to do what we call *predictive analytics*."

Moe was clearly in his element by now. "This is the part of the plan that excites me the most. I know, this is all still theory and I haven't done it myself. But I'm feeling confident that we're on the right track."

Moe looked a far cry from the shaky and hesitant squirrel Aly had met earlier. "And don't worry. I know this seems too much to take in. It's our job to explain all this and clear all your doubts."

Doubts? Yes, I have plenty. "You'd better do so!"

"Aly, you look like you could really do with a break," Moe said. "It's probably a good time too, as I'll need Fab to join us from this point on. Let's come back in the afternoon."

Does this kid ever listen?! "Moe, you're testing my patience! You don't call the shots here. Haven't I made it clear?!"

"You did," Moe said. "I'm sorry, and I promise that there will be no one else. But trust me, you're going to love what we're going to do next. We're just getting started."

Chapter 5
Explore

"ALY, YOU NEED to look at this!" Lex was gasping as he approached Moe's burrow. He had been desperately trying to find Aly's whereabouts, finally figuring that he had to be at Moe's. He knew very well what had been keeping Aly busy lately.

Lex had decided to distance himself from Aly, Moe, and their plans. He was especially furious that Aly had let Moe make decisions about the mining team at his expense. But he was beginning to tone down his stance, accepting that both he and Aly had done all they could and it was time to look for unconventional alternatives. What was happening now, though, was making him think twice.

"DON'T TRY TO BE CLEVER…," read a note that he was holding. "OR YOU ARE IN DEEP TROUBLE."

"This came from Maq," Lex said. "One of his miners passed this note to one of ours in the maze. This was just earlier today."

Moe was fidgeting in his chair. "Is this a threat?" he asked with a shaky voice.

"What else?!" Lex slammed the burrow's door shut. "And it's all because of you, kid! They must've noticed our miners behaving strangely in the past week with all this scanning business."

"And now Maq has issued this warning," Aly said, seemingly in deep thought.

Lex wasn't going to keep his displeasure to himself. "And that means it's not safe for my miners anymore. How can I ever let them go into the maze again? This is all turning into a bigger mess!"

Lex couldn't help but feel victorious. He had wanted to get back at Moe, and now, he was winning the battle. *Kid, you have no idea how much misery you've been causing me.*

"Just hang on a second. And take a step back,"

Aly said, to Lex's surprise. Aly appeared unruffled by what he had just heard.

Is he still going ahead? Lex thought.

"Lex, you know Maq," Aly said. "He's ruthless and cold-blooded. But for all that, has he actually ever set out to harm us?"

Lex was quiet. He knew the answer.

Aly looked assured. "You know they won't go that far. Will they play rough in the maze to gain the advantage? Yes, they already do. But will they intentionally set about hurting our miners? I don't think so."

"But what makes you think he won't do it this time?" Lex challenged Aly, trying to change his opinion. "He's smart enough to notice that we're up to something."

Aly smiled confidently. "You know Maq," he said. "All he's interested in is staying in power. Guess what will happen if he starts to wreak havoc in the maze? There will be a revolt. Massive revolt. Clans will be fighting each other. That's never a good thing for a leader like him. He needs stability if he wants to stay in charge."

What magic spell has this kid put on you? "So what do you make of this threat then?" Lex asked, raising his voice.

"I see the opposite."

Lex took a quick step back. "What do you mean?"

"I see that he is scared," Aly said. "And this is just his way of channeling his fears in the hope that we take the bait and bow out. This is normal."

He then took out a small, worn notebook, scribbled something on it, which Lex could just about get a glimpse of.

Reminder to self: When you start doing something different, others take notice. Some go to the extent of blocking your progress. That's when you know you're on the right track.

Aly's notes

By now, Aly seemed to be dropping wisdom with every word that he uttered.

For a fleeting moment, though, he gazed downward and looked perturbed. "But here's the bigger thing. The fact that they're scared means only one thing will happen. They'll send even more miners into the maze and work extra hard to get their share of nuts. Guys, it's not getting any easier from now on."

He suddenly rose from his chair. "And that's why it's even more important that we go ahead with the plan. We simply don't have any other choice."

Easy for you to say! "That means you're going to put our miners' safety at risk!" Lex said.

"Lex, I'm not saying we ignore this threat. Our miners' safety will always be at the top of my concern."

Aly then spelled out a few changes he wanted to see. "Starting today, the miners must be more alert to their surroundings. Send them in pairs if necessary. If they fear for their safety at night, then we'll not send as many miners during those times. I'm willing to take a hit on the collection of nuts no matter how excruciating that is."

Lex knew that he couldn't change Aly's mind. Aly had already decided.

"In fact," Aly said, "put me on the mining shift for the next couple of days."

For a few seconds, deafening silence pervaded the room. Lex couldn't believe what he was hearing.

"It's been many years since my mining days,"

Aly said, "but now, I'm going back in. We'll use this period to gauge the maze."

With the new standard that Aly had just set, Lex couldn't do anything else but comply. "From now on," Lex said, "I'll ask the miners to give frequent reports on what happened in the maze. We'll also need to keep tweaking our plans. For example, having to send fewer miners at certain times, depending on situations. Do I get your approval for that?"

In truth, though, Lex was just paying lip service. His mind was elsewhere.

"Yes, you have my full trust," Aly said. "We have no other option now. We have to be more selective."

Out of the blue, Moe said, "In fact, soon, being selective will not be out of necessity but choice."

"How is that going to be possible?" Lex asked, smirking.

"I can tell you how… if you let me continue my discussion with Aly."

"Moe, Lex is now part of the team. He'll join us," Aly said.

"Sure," Moe said. "He's more than welcome.

Now let's start."

* * *

Rather than bringing him down, Maq's threatening note had, instead, reinvigorated Aly. Privately, he took it as a validation that they were heading in the right direction. *Surely, we must be doing something right if Maq is taking notice?*

After all, the threat had shoved him into a path where there really was no other choice than to see the plan through. *I must give my full trust to Moe. We will give it our all.* "Tell me, what do we need to do now?" he asked Moe.

Moe signaled to Bob to take over the discussion and he duly began. "Remember where we left off? We're now ready to dive further into the data. We'll look at it in different ways. Then look for more patterns and signs."

"That doesn't sound any different from the one we had discussed," Aly said. "Isn't that the same as descriptive analytics?"

"Great question," Bob said. "The answer is yes and no, though. It's a yes because we're analyzing the same historical data. But that's where the similarities end. The difference is, this time, we're looking at the data with a different purpose, which is to predict the future."

"Predict the future? How are we going to do that?" Lex looked intrigued by what he was hearing. Coming late into the picture, he was naturally behind in understanding what they were trying to do. But Aly was pleased, seeing that Lex was beginning to be involved in the discussion.

"We do that by exploring the data," Bob answered. "We find what features are the most useful and how to use them when we do the predictions later. This is when we try to link our earlier observations about the data with the reasons *why* they happened."

"We call this *exploratory data analysis*," Bob said as he wrote those words on the drawing board. "For example, we may discover that we won't need all of the features to do a good prediction after all. On the contrary, we may find that the features are not conclusive enough, so we may need to collect data on other features."

"And this is where I'll let Fab take over," Moe said.

In many ways, Fab was like Moe. The clan

knew Moe for his inventions, and the same went for Fab. Both liked to experiment and build nifty little tools that they took great satisfaction from.

But, unlike the controversial Moe, he was a very likable figure within the clan. Some squirrels called him "The Brain." He was good at mathematics and loved to teach the other squirrels too, especially the young ones. They loved him due to his knack for explaining seemingly complex math concepts into something they could relate to.

"Let's now look at the data," Fab began. "First, recall the features that we have. We have those about the nuts: miner's name, date, time, location, type of nut, and amount."

"And we have those about the environment: temperature, humidity, and brightness. Nothing too complicated." Fab oozed calm and ease when he spoke, giving Aly a much-needed boost of optimism.

Name	Date	Time (hr)	Location (sub-zone)	Type	Temp (° F)	Humidity (RH %)	Brightness (lx)	Amount (grams)
Ben	25-Feb	13:00	Zone 5 - West	Almond	90	42	420	8
Ben	25-Feb	07:00	Zone 6 - North East	Pistachio	56	56	120	2
Nat	25-Feb	10:00	Zone 7 - Central	Pecan	75	32	250	5
Wim	25-Feb	21:00	Zone 3 - South East	Pistachio	58	40	5	1
...	...	...	...	...	...	...	...	...
...	...	...	...	...	...	...	...	...
...	...	...	...	...	...	...	...	...
...	...	...	...	...	...	...	...	...

"Exploratory data analysis," Fab said, "is about finding out those few features that best predict the outcome."

"Slow down a bit. I didn't get that," Aly said.

Fab smiled and nodded. "Let's put it another way," he said. "If you were allowed to pick only one feature to help you find more nuts, which one would it be?"

"Probably the location," Aly said.

"What made you choose that?" Fab asked.

"Because we've seen that nuts showed up more at certain locations than in the others."

Fab smiled. "Good point, but there's one problem with that. You're limiting your observations to just the symptoms. When you found more nuts at certain locations and times, those were just symptoms. A result of something else."

"But we haven't really understood the *cause*," he continued. "The reason *why* it happened. That's why we should check out the other features."

"You mean, those features about the environment?" Aly asked.

"Yes," Fab said. "There must be a reason why we see more nuts at certain locations and times than the others, and those features may give us some clues."

"What exactly are we looking for?" Lex asked. He was starting to be more engaged, looking genuinely curious.

"Correlations."

Lex looked befuddled at yet another foreign term. "I have no clue what you're talking about."

"Lex, we're in the same boat," Aly said.

Fab chuckled. "I'll explain. Let's take one example, humidity. We need to find out if more nuts appeared in the more humid places. If that turns out to be true, we will have found a strong correlation."

"What if we found the opposite?" Lex asked. "I mean, what if more nuts appeared in drier places instead?"

Why didn't I think of that? Aly thought.

"Great observation," Fab said. "That's a correlation too, in the opposite direction."

"Now, what if both were true?" Lex pushed further. "Let's say, of the top ten places with the most nuts, some were humid and some were dry."

"When that happens," Fab said, "it means you've got a weak or even no correlation. It means that you wouldn't have much success predicting the outcome from that feature. You move on and analyze the next one."

"Interesting," Aly said. "Now tell me, Fab, what did you manage to find? Did you see any correlations in our data?"

"I did, and it wasn't humidity. Instead, I saw a fairly strong correlation between the amount of nuts and temperature."

"You mean, the warmer the place, the more nuts would appear there?" Aly felt a light bulb coming on in his head. *This is really going somewhere*, he thought.

"Yes," Fab said. "Those places with the most nuts were among the warmest last week."

"Interesting! We're making progress. Did you find any other correlations?" Aly continued to probe.

"I did," Fab said. "A close second was brightness. I found that the brighter the place was, the chance of finding more nuts was higher."

Aly's eyes widened. "Oh wow! It makes sense to me now. That explains why we always see more nuts in the daytime."

"It needs to be a bright day, of course," Fab said. "If it's cloudy throughout, chances are it'll be a gloomy day for the miners, quite literally!"

"What a waste," Aly said. "We were never able to explain these patterns, so we ignored them. If only we knew this much earlier. But on the bright side, it seems we're on course to crack this problem!"

> There are insights hidden within the data waiting to be uncovered.
>
> Aly's notes

"Here's the best part," Fab said. "We can also get the computer to find these correlations for us."

"You mean, the computer can figure out all these correlations automatically?" Lex looked perplexed.

Fab smiled. "Yes. I had simplified this example just so you could grasp its basic concept. But really, a lot more math and computing need to go into it. Which I'll spare you from!"

Aly burst out laughing. "Good move!"

"Okay, jokes aside," Fab continued. "In reality, it will usually be a combination of both. That's why it's still imperative that we do our own exploratory data analysis and only then get the computer to complement it. Let me be clear; we simply cannot skip that."

"Fine, I hear you," Aly said. "Now, all this looks nice and it feels like we're making progress. But still, we haven't answered the big question yet. How can we use the data to tell what will happen in the coming weeks?"

"I know," Moe said, "you can't get your mind off the idea of a computer training and learning, right? That's what we're going to do next!"

"Yes, and more than that. We need to see results. Period," Aly said.

"Sure!" Moe said. "In the next step, we'll use

what we've learned from exploring the data. Once that's done, we're ready to deploy our plan. Now that the hard part is out of the way, let's get to the fun stuff."

Chapter 6
Model

LEX'S PULSE CONTINUED to rise the longer he was in the room. His limbs were shaking and he couldn't sit still because when he had brought the threatening note to Aly earlier, he only told half the story.

What he didn't tell Aly was that Maq had also given him a private message. Maq had asked him to spy on Aly should he decide to ignore the threat and continue with the plan. In return, he had promised Lex the role as head of his mining team and, with that, a seal of approval to join his clan.

Now that Aly had decided to press ahead, Lex was left in a conundrum. He was torn between his loyalty to Gliff and his own well-being.

He knew Gliff's future was as bleak as it had ever been. They simply couldn't survive if they continued to mine in the same way. But on the flip side, if they changed their ways and then succeeded, Maq and the other clans would be breathing down their necks. *We're trapped either way.*

He knew, once Maq got his way, Gliff's chances of escaping from their plight were next to nothing. *I don't have a choice.* Still unsure of his stance, he had reluctantly started on this spy mission by pretending to be engaged in the discussions. But as Aly and the team were about to resume, he finally decided.

If you can't beat them, join them.

Aly had noticed that Lex wasn't being his usual self. Yes, the threat was real, and you'd be lucky to find someone who could display composure during such times. But he was irritatingly forceful at times, looked extremely attentive for one moment and was disengaged the next. *Poor squirrel. Maybe the pressure is getting to him.*

"We're now going to shift another gear," Fab

said. We're going to the fourth step of our plan, and it's called *modeling*. Let's start by revisiting what our goal was."

Fab moved toward the drawing board with the pen at the ready. "What we want to know is *for each hour of the day, which locations will give us the most nuts?*"

"It points us to the single thing we're trying to predict," Moe said.

I think I know this one, Aly thought. "We want to predict the amount of nuts at a given location and hour. Am I right?"

"Spot on!" Moe said. "We call this the *target variable*."

Aly looked across at Lex. "Do you agree, Lex? This is your forte."

No answer.

"Lex? Are you okay?"

"Oh, sorry." Lex turned around to Aly as if being woken up from a dream. "Yes, what did you just say?"

"Do you agree on our goal?" Aly said, pointing to the board.

"Yes, yes. Sure, agreed."

"Great," Fab said. "That is what the computer will attempt to learn and predict. It's never going to be one hundred percent accurate, but we can make it very close."

"But first, let me give an analogy," Moe said. "Imagine baby squirrels learning to become good at climbing trees."

"Okay, what about it?" Aly asked.

"When they're starting out," Moe said, "you would guide them by showing the dos and don'ts, the rights and wrongs. Right?"

"Right."

"They'll use that and then learn even more after doing it themselves. They'll go through a lot of trials and errors, and finally, they get better over time."

Nothing new, Aly thought.

"Then the time finally comes when they have become fairly good at what they're doing. What do you do then?" Moe asked.

"You would test them?" Aly guessed.

"Right. You test them to see if they're ready."

But what is he trying to get at?

"And once they're ready," Moe said, "they'll go out there and use what they've learned. Over time, they'll accumulate even more experience, learn even more, and get even better."

Aly continued to play along, still struggling to understand what parallels Moe was trying to explain. *That was just common sense. What's so special about it? And what does it have to do with the computer?*

Moe went to the board again and wrote something. "The computer learns in exactly the same way. We call this *machine learning.*"

Aly's eyes widened. He wasn't accepting this. "No way! How can that be?" *Is he saying there is a squirrel inside the computer?!*

"Don't worry," Moe said, "you'll understand once you see it in action. This concept is at the heart of our plan, so we're not going anywhere until you're comfortable with it. Fab, go ahead."

"Sure," Fab said. "First, let's go back to the data that we had collected. Did you notice how many data points were there?"

"Yes, 10,000," Aly said.

"Correct. From this, we'll take 7,000 data points, or 70 percent, to train the computer. We'll call this the training dataset."

Aly didn't get any of that. "What does that even mean?"

Fab raised his paw in apology, apparently noticing he went too fast. "Training means, for each data point, we'll feed the computer with the inputs and what the correct output is supposed to be."

"Let me guess," Lex asked out of the blue. "The inputs would be all the features, and the output would be the target variable." He'd been quiet but suddenly came alive.

"Exactly!" Fab said.

Okay, now I think I get it. "Is it like giving the computer the question and telling it what the answer is?" Aly asked.

Fab beamed. "Yes, you can put it that way too. I like that analogy."

By now, Lex was vigorously taking notes, a lot of them.

I like this, Aly smiled. *Good that he's finally on board with the team.*

"Examples always help," Fab said, pointing to the computer screen. He switched the view to display a table. "Let's take this one data point in the east of Zone 4. On Wednesday, between 5 and 6 p.m., the target variable was 100 grams, and we have the corresponding value for each of humidity, brightness, and temperature. This data point, like each of the other 6,999, has its own insight about how the target variable is correlated to the different features."

Still sitting in front of the screen, Fab turned back toward Aly and Lex. "To put it simply, the computer's job is to find patterns and insights from all the training data points put together."

"But wait," Lex said. "Why do we need the computer to help us understand the data? We can explore the data ourselves. That's exactly what we just did earlier!"

"You're right," Fab said. "But that's only because we were dealing with a small dataset and observing for only general patterns. The question is, can we do that on a much bigger scale and still capture the finer details? We can't."

Fab opened his arms wide, giving an effect of holding a giant ball. "Imagine having a huge amount of data for the whole of the maze coming every week over the course of many months. It'll have seasonal effects, invalid data points, and inconsistent patterns that we need to sift through and make sense of each. Every single time."

"Or what if we added more features to the data?" Moe added. "Let's say ten times what we have now. We squirrels just wouldn't be able to handle it!"

Moe continued. "That's why we have the computer, also known as the machine, to do all the learning on our behalf. As Fab just said, they can do all these computations that are impossible for us."

"Okay, I get the point," Lex said.

Still, this doesn't feel complete, Aly thought. "So, we've now told the machine *what* to learn. That part is fine," he said. "But then, *how* does it actually learn? There must be a brain somewhere!"

Moe took a deep breath and let the discussion take a slower pace for a while. They had covered quite a bit and Fab had done a good job of running the discussion. And since Fab was doing most of the talking, Moe had found more time to observe. So, it didn't escape him that Lex had been behaving strangely. *Something isn't right about him.*

"It's called an *algorithm*," Moe said. "That's the 'brain' of the machine."

Moe giggled as Aly and Lex looked at each other in bewilderment. "Don't worry. It's not that scary once you understand the principle. Algorithms are step-by-step mathematical calculations that represent how the machine thinks and makes decisions. These algorithms, in fact, many of them, are already available for you to choose from."

Moe paused just to let that sink in. "And depending on the goals that you want to achieve, you choose the most appropriate algorithm. The same way that learning to climb a tree and learning to mine nuts are two totally different skills that need to be learned in different ways, which require different 'algorithms' in our brain."

"So, let me get this right," Aly said. "The machine will learn using the algorithm that we will select?"

"Correct, and it's perfectly fine to try out a few algorithms and compare," Moe said.

"Okay, clear," Lex said. "Now let's move faster, can we? Tell me, what happens when training is done?" he demanded, clearly now in a hurry. That irked Fab, and it didn't bode well with Aly either.

"Lex!" Aly said. "This is by far the most crucial part of the plan. I must understand how it works if I'm ever going to approve it. I trust Fab knows how to pace it right. If you could let him continue..."

Lex didn't say a word and looked away, frowning.

"No problems, let's continue," Fab said, looking slightly uncomfortable with the tension that was building. "To answer your question, Lex, once the training is done, we've got ourselves a *model*."

"A model is simply an algorithm that's been tuned," Moe said.

"Tuned?" Aly asked.

"Yes," Moe said. "Tuned according to the training dataset and the goal it wants to achieve."

"So, what happens after that?" Aly asked.

"The model be will be considered ready."

"Ready for...?"

"Testing," Moe answered. "It's the step we've been waiting for. By having the model available, the computer is now trained and ready to be tested."

"Okay," Aly said, "I suppose the reason you left out the other 30 percent of the dataset was to save it for testing. Right?"

"Well done!" Fab said. "During testing, we'll do the reverse of training. We'll feed the computer with the features of each data point, but not the target variable."

"Giving the question but not the answer!" Aly said, reminding about the metaphor he had brought up earlier.

"Correct," Fab said. "The job of the computer now is to use the inputs, which are the features, to predict the output, which is the target variable."

"Oh!" Aly raised both his arms up as if he had just found his eureka moment. "That means now we can compare the actual target variable with what the model had predicted."

"Pretty neat, isn't it?" Moe said. "For example, out of the 3,000 test data points, if 2,700 were predicted accurately, that means the model would be 90 percent accurate."

> The machine learns very much like we do. It ultimately learns the most by gathering experience, through many attempts, and getting better over time.
>
> Aly's notes

Fab then went on to draw a diagram on the board. "Let's now try to firm up our understanding. During training, the machine will use the features and target variable from the training dataset to build the model."

He then drew another diagram. "Then, during testing, the machine will use the model that it had built and the features from the test dataset to predict the target variable."

"Sorry for being rude just now," Lex said. "But thanks. It'll take time to digest, but that was enlightening. It feels like we're giving the machine the intelligence to help us do things in a much better way."

"Intelligence! That's the word," Fab said.

"Though we're not doing that for now, we can actually train the machine to give us not just predictions on 'what will happen' but also recommendations on 'what action we should take'. We call this *prescriptive analytics,* and this is bordering on the realm of what we call *artificial intelligence.*"

"In fact," he continued, "with artificial intelligence, we can take it one step further by getting the machine to actually perform specific, clearly-defined tasks based on those predictions and recommendations."

"Um, really?" Lex asked. "You mean, like mining the nuts?"

Fab smiled and said, "Don't be surprised if one day you see robo-squirrels going into the maze, learning about it, and yes, mining the nuts!"

Moe could see both excitement and disbelief in the faces of Aly and Lex, at which point, he signaled Fab to move on.

"But let's not get carried away, nor should we be worried about it," Fab said. "It's not that straightforward and it's still a long way before that could happen. What I wanted to show was that artificial intelligence and data science are coming from the same foundation. Though their applications can be totally contrasting, they are both possible because of machine learning, and most importantly, data."

"I'm starting to love this," Aly said. "And I want to know more! Can you explain other ways we can use machine learning for the benefit of our clan? I mean, things we can do today, not in the future," he asked.

"I can tell you of another one, which in fact we are already using. It's the nut scanner." Moe said. "Remember? You weren't convinced that it could tell the type of nuts just by scanning them."

"I was," Aly said, "but to be honest, I don't have issues with that anymore! I tested it out at home with different nuts and it worked like magic. Pretty accurate."

Moe beamed. "That was possible because of machine learning too," he said. "I trained the scanner to be able to tell the type of nut from the image that it scanned."

Aly crossed his arms and leaned back. "But how is that machine learning? Those are images, not numbers."

"That's the power of math," Fab said, ever the

math enthusiast. "We can turn almost everything around us into data, be it *structured data* like our nuts collection table, or *unstructured data* like images, texts, speeches, movements, and more. Once we've done that, we can start applying machine learning to the data."

> The machine can turn almost everything around us into data. And from there, we can get it to learn and make predictions on our behalf.
>
> Aly's notes

"There you have it," Moe said. "You may have not noticed, but now you've already seen two of the most common types of machine learning models. You saw the first one with the nuts predictions. We were trying to answer the question of 'how much?', and it's a type of model we call *regression*."

Moe cleared his throat and gave some time for Aly and Lex to digest that, before continuing, "With the nut scanner, we're trying to answer a different kind of question, which is 'what type is it?'. This model is called *classification*."

"Hold on there," Aly said. "Why don't I run by you how I think the nut scanner works? Then you tell me if I'm getting the hang of all this."

Moe was pleasantly surprised. "Sure! Go ahead."

"First," Aly began, "using the scanner, we collect a dataset of many different nut images and feed it into the computer."

Moe nodded. *Doing well so far.*

"Then," Aly continued, "we set aside a portion of the dataset for training and pick a suitable algorithm. We'll get the computer to learn by revealing the correct type of nut for each image."

Impressive, Moe thought, giving the thumbs up.

"And with that," Aly said, "you would have tuned your algorithm and gotten yourself a working model. You can now put the scanner to test. It will tell you what type of nut it is just by scanning it. This is turning out to be quite fun!"

Moe pressed his paws together and bowed to Aly. "Looks like you're starting to think like a data scientist."

"Data scientist? What's that?" Aly asked.

"That's what Fab is!"

Chapter 7
Tune

"SIXTY-EIGHT?! THAT'S unacceptable!" Aly stared at the number on the screen, feeling like they were going back to square one. Reality was so different from theory, it seemed. Images of his clan getting dragged further into suffering started to rush back into his mind. *So much for all the optimism!*

Moe and Fab were now showing him the training and test results. They had explained that for this type of algorithm, the best way to define its accuracy was using an *error* value. This error value would give the average difference, in grams, between the predicted and actual amounts of nuts at a particular date, hour, and location.

After much deliberation, Aly, Lex, Moe, and

Fab had arrived at an agreed measure of the model's accuracy. An average error value of ten or less would indicate that the model had a good accuracy and would be ready to be deployed. A model with an average error value of between ten to fifty was defined as average, whereas anything beyond fifty would mean a model with poor accuracy.

The training dataset had given a respectable error value of five. But sixty-eight for the test dataset did not inspire any confidence, to say the least. "How can we possibly deploy this model? It will tell me that there could be sixty-eight grams of nuts even if there were none!" Aly banged his fist on the table, unable to contain his frustration.

Moe, who was standing across the room, didn't say a word. He was clearly trying to avoid eye contact with Aly. "Um, I, I think something is wrong somewhere," he stammered. "I can't point to it precisely right now, but it's quite normal to have such gaps in accuracy between the training and test datasets."

Fab, who had seemed to be deep in thought, then said, "It's, indeed, normal."

Aly could literally hear Moe's relief, such a

loud sigh it was.

"When we see this kind of scenario, it indicates a problem of *overfitting*," Fab said. "Overfitting happens when the accuracy in testing turns out to be much worse than in training."

"Nice sounding term," Lex groused. "But the only thing I'm interested in is how to fix this problem!"

"Lex, please, let Fab explain," Aly said, starting to come to his senses. He knew Fab was onto something and didn't want Lex to spoil it with his impatience.

"Sure," Fab said. "Overfitting happens when the model has captured a bit too much information from the training dataset, making it poor at adapting to future data. A good model must have a good balance of both."

"Okay then," Aly said. "Now, going back to Lex's point, how do we use this to fix the model?"

"There are many ways," Fab said. "But let's look at one."

For a while, Fab stared down at the floor and then turned toward Aly with an apologetic look. "First, I must admit that we shouldn't have waited until now to consider them. We should've done so when we trained our model the first time around. I guess I was too hasty to see the outcome myself. My bad."

"Don't worry," Aly said. "Admitting one's mistake is a hallmark of a great squirrel too, provided you make sure this is fixed soon, of course!" Aly had cooled down, confident that Fab would get this back on track. *He's a normal squirrel after all.*

"I'll do my best! Now let's look at it. With the benefit of hindsight, we should have introduced *regularization* while training the model."

"Regularization is quite a simple concept, and it's all about achieving what Fab had explained: balance," Moe said, seeming to have recovered from the earlier setback. "It helps the model find the right balance by learning just enough from the training data. Neither too little nor too much."

Fab said, "The moment you read too much into the training dataset, the more you're 'memorizing' it. That's when the problem starts. You always want to learn, not memorize."

"Okay," Aly said. "All these sounds cool conceptually, but how does the computer know how to do this?"

"It's taken care of by the math. That's all you need to know," Fab said, smiling.

Aly chuckled. "Perfect!"

"So, are we done?" Lex asked. "If that's all we need to do to fix the model, then let's do it now."

"Not yet," Fab said. "We'll still need to make a few more changes. For example, we'll do more cross-validations, which means that we're splitting the dataset into smaller chunks, then repeating training and testing a few more times using different combinations of these chunks. This will help to improve our model."

"Training the model differently is not the only way to improve it," Moe said. "We can also make changes to the data itself."

"Like adding more data?" Lex asked.

"Yes," Fab said, "if you have the time and resources to collect more data, of course. In our case, we don't. But we have other ways, such as removing certain features that aren't as useful or removing data points that we deem as bad."

"Okay, I think that's a good place to stop," Aly said. "I trust that you know what you're doing. Now let's retrain the model and see the outcome. We really don't have any more time."

* * *

Moe's eyes lit up looking at what Fab was showing on the screen. They had spent a much longer time retraining the model than training it the first time. As the clock was ticking away, he knew this was his and Gliff's last chance to find something to give them hope. "Guys, I think you'll like what I'm seeing."

"Wait," Lex said. "I'm still not convinced. Maybe we're just being lucky. I don't want us to wing it once but fail miserably at the very next attempt."

Moe was unsure about Lex's motive. "What are you getting at? What do you want us to do?"

"I want to be sure that our fundamentals are right. I want you to explain the whole plan again and convince us that it's sound enough. Agreed, Aly?"

Aly nodded. "I would rather move faster but I have to agree with Lex," he said. "He wasn't around when we discussed the first few steps. So, it's only fair to him that we do it. Besides, I think I need a review myself!"

"If that's what you want," Moe said, "I'm

more than happy to do it. In fact, we do have a little bit of time while the computer is running its final calculations."

Moe didn't have any issue with the request. But something about Lex's body language was telling him that something wasn't right somewhere. *Focus, Moe. Nothing's wrong.* "Let's start. Altogether, our plan is called data science, and it's made up of five steps."

Moe then turned to Aly and said, "If you remember, in the beginning, we weren't even talking about the data. Instead, we worked together to nail down the problem to be solved and *define* our goal. That was step one."

"Make sense," Aly said. "Now I know why you were asking me all those questions about our mining operations."

"That's right," Moe said. "I cannot overstate how vital this part is. You get it wrong here, and everything that follows will just mislead you into thinking you're making progress."

> Data science doesn't work if you just sit in front of the screen and work on your models. You need go out there and nail down the problem to be solved.
>
> Aly's notes

"Then…," Moe continued, "once that was out of the way, we moved to step two, *data collection*. This was when I brought Gil in, who was really good at not just identifying the right data to collect, but also cleaning and organizing them in the best possible way."

"I underestimated that part," Aly said. "I thought it was going to be a breeze. We ended up spending most of our time cleaning and organizing the data. Gil had done a thankless job behind the scenes. She did great."

Moe had noticed Lex writing down whatever he said word for word. He was much more attentive than he had been before. *I'll never get along with him. But, at least, he seems eager to learn.*

"Now, onto step three, *data analysis*," Moe said. "This was when Bob did descriptive analytics to summarize what had happened."

"Which was when we found out about the

Mystery Zone," Aly said.

Yes, that fluke. "Yes, that one. And, um, I know, we haven't got back to you with further analysis on that yet. But what we really wanted to know in this step was why more nuts were found in certain places than in the others. That was when Fab took us through exploratory data analysis."

"Correlations, I remember!" Aly said.

"Yes," Moe said. "We found that temperature and brightness were the biggest clues to help us predict the amount of nuts that will appear."

"And that's when we moved to step four, *modeling,* didn't we?" Aly interjected.

"You're right," Moe said. "Fab explained about machine learning, where we built a model to predict the amount of nuts at a given time and location."

"This was when my head went a bit fuzzy," Lex said. "How did we build the model again?"

"First, all the model had was an algorithm. We then ran our training dataset through the model, letting it know the correct value of the target variable for each data point. This was when the model learned about the relationship between the features and the target variable."

"Got it now," Lex said. "Then the testing part came, which failed."

He's getting on my nerves again. Moe was infuriated by Lex's rashness but knew he couldn't let his temper ruin this progress. "We didn't really fail. We just had to go back and tune our model. Yes, data science is amazing. But make no mistake, we still need to put in the effort to make it work. And Fab has done exactly that. Fab, please."

"Sure," Fab said. "If you remember, our model was overfitted. Since then, we've made a few changes and retrained the model."

"What's the new error value then? Are we ready?" Lex asked.

"Yes, we are," Fab said. "It's seven."

Aly's fists punched the air. "Seven? Finally!"

"Which means that the model is now doing extremely well!" Moe couldn't stop feeling a sense of pride, having reached such a key moment. "That sets us up nicely for the fifth and final step of our data science plan. This is the only step we haven't seen in action yet, but now it's the right time to—"

"No time for that one, Moe," Aly said. "Now that we know the model's working, what are we waiting for? Deploy it! From today onwards, our mining plans and decisions will be solely guided by the predictions from the model."

Moe looked across at Fab, who simply shrugged his shoulders.

"Sure," Lex said. "I'll keep everyone posted on our progress."

"Thanks, Lex. Please work closely with Moe and his team. It's time to be selective. It's time to be clever. No more running around like headless chickens. Listen to what the model says, and I have no doubt that we'll succeed."

Chapter 8
Redefine

TWO WEEKS PASSED and the Gliffs were in dreamland. The nut collection was almost twice as much compared to the same period before that. Aly couldn't have envisioned such a swift turnaround of fortune. But more than anything, the newfound hope rippling through Gliff was what he savored the most. The mood within the clan had been completely uplifted. *This place feels totally different now. I can't thank Moe enough.*

Moe's team had been fully embedded into the mining team, working closely together. The mining operations were improving by the day as more data was collected and the machine learning models were updated. Each morning, his team would produce a report detailing the predicted locations and times with the most nuts, which was then turned into a mining plan.

As part of his role, each day, Bob would monitor the nut collection data closely. After all, Bob was the cool "Insights Nut" as he was now known among the team, being remarkably good at using different kinds of visualizations and analysis on the computer to detect interesting patterns.

But that morning, he looked unmistakably anxious. As Aly and Moe were entering the mining operations headquarters, they couldn't help but notice this strange behavior.

"He looks tense," Moe said. "This is so unlike Bob. He's the calmest squirrel I know. Something must be terribly wrong."

"Let's talk to him," Aly said as they walked toward Bob.

"Hey, Bob," Moe said. "What's up? Is everything okay? Looks like something's bothering you."

"Um, actually… yes," Bob said hesitantly. "This data is telling me something really worrying."

Moe's eyes widened. "What's that?"

Bob scrubbed his paw over his face. "The past three days' collection is slowing down. And looking at the trend, it will only go down further."

Aly didn't blink looking at a chart that Bob was showing on the screen. "But why is this happening all of a sudden?"

Bob looked downcast. "It's something the miners have noticed recently and it's now finally showing in the data," he said. "The other clans were trailing them to every spot they went to. Every time they looked back, there would always be one or two who were waiting and making the same moves and turns that our miners made."

Bob's shoulders slumped as he continued, "And, of course, the moment nuts came out around that spot, the other miners would dash in and get to the nuts first before our miners could get their paws on them."

"That's creepy," Moe said.

"Actually, not at all," Aly said. "They're stronger and bigger in numbers, but make no mistake, they're smart too."

"That's true," Bob said. "They would have noticed how our miners have been doing their jobs differently now. They would have asked why we weren't running around anymore and, instead, making these calculated moves."

"And for sure," Aly said, "they would have noticed our collection bags being fuller than usual."

"So, over the past couple of weeks," Bob said, "they've figured out that we could anticipate when and where the nuts would come out. They then followed in our footsteps, literally!"

Moe gave a long sigh. "And in these situations, it comes back to the numbers and strength that they have, and they'll beat us every time. We're back to square one."

Bob was clearly trying to avoid eye contact. "I'm afraid so. Sorry that I didn't let you know about this earlier. I've been looking hard into the data and listening from the miners for the last couple of days, and it's only now that I can be sure of this."

A long silence accentuated the background noise coming from the mining operations headquarters.

"Don't give up just yet. Because I think now is the time," Aly said out of the blue.

"Time for what?" Moe asked.

"For us to meet the other clans."

Never mind Moe and Bob, even Aly himself couldn't believe what he was saying. *What are we going to meet them for? To ask for sympathy and let us have some of their food? Forget it.*

"Um, Aly, are you sure?" Moe asked. "I think our predecessors have tried that many times with no success. These clans are so selfish that all they think about is their own needs and wants."

Then something clicked in Aly's mind. He knew he had a hunch about something, but he just couldn't explain it. "Moe, remember what you told me last time? That there could be way more nuts than needed out there."

Aly was just letting his instincts tell him what to say. "I'm changing my mind now. I'm agreeing with you. What if that were true? What if there were a surplus even after all the clans had taken their shares."

"It's strange that we're reversing roles here," Moe said. "I know I brought it up at that time. But, to be honest, I was really just regurgitating old tales and mysteries, which are good stories to tell, but have no basis whatsoever."

Aly jolted from his chair. Something about

what Moe had just said triggered something in his mind. *Mysteries?! Of course! Thanks, Moe!*

Aly felt a rush of adrenaline as he contemplated what he was about to attempt. "I know our predecessors had tried it and failed. But, this time, we'll go back to them and convince them... in a different way."

"But how do you plan to do that?" Bob asked.

"If we start talking about letting us have some of their nuts because they don't need all of them, it won't go anywhere. Not the same old stuff," Aly said.

"Then, what are we going to talk about?" Moe asked.

Aly rubbed his paws together. "We need to talk about something that transcends everything that we at Nutancia had ever done before."

"Aly, this is making me nervous," Moe said. "Somehow, I feel I'll be dragged into this also. Tell me, what are you thinking about?"

"Moe, imagine if you were the leader of a clan," Aly said. "What if I came to you with a proposition, one that clearly shows what's in it for your clan? Better still, one that offers something more. Something they've never had before. You would at least listen, right?"

"I guess so."

"And that's precisely what we're going to do."

"And how are we going to do that?" Moe asked.

Aly winked. "Using data, of course! But we need Lex. Where's Lex?"

It had taken Lex longer than expected and he still felt far from ready, but he knew he had to draw courage from somewhere. Maq had instructed him to give a full dossier of what Moe and his team were up to. But Lex had always had a grudge against Moe, and he had never really put his heart into the plan. So, he struggled to keep up no matter how much notes he took. When it came to deploying the miners, he was just blindly following the predictions from Moe's machine learning models. But he knew Maq was getting impatient.

Maq was intimidating even when he smiled, which was rare, so when Lex saw him limbering up his shoulders and cracking his knuckles from afar, he felt like turning back.

"You're too late. We've figured it out ourselves."

"I'm sorry," Lex said, his paws trembling. "It took me a longer time to figure things out. You know it's not easy to—"

"Give me results, not excuses. So, what do you have for me?"

"I can send you reports every day. The same reports that Moe is giving me. This way, you can—"

"Is that all that you've got?!" Maq was almost screaming. "It's not enough. I don't settle for second best. I don't play catch up with the Gliffs. I want to be ahead of the curve."

"Um, what are you trying to say?"

"You go figure it out yourself."

"But what about your promise?" Lex asked. "When are you going to bring me into your team?"

"I won't, unless you bring me what I want. I want the same knowledge that Moe has. I expect you to build our own data science team here!"

"But I don't know if that's ever going to be possible," Lex said. "Moe didn't just learn it overnight. And if he couldn't, what makes you think I can?"

Maq fixed his glare at Lex. "That's your job. I don't want to know how you do it, but you will do it. It's not an option!"

* * *

Aly could see the puzzled look in Moe's face. Aly couldn't stop smiling, thinking how far they'd come. *I'm learning from you, Moe.* He knew what he was about to embark on was such a tall order, but right now, fear was the last thing in his mind.

"Moe, remember the Mystery Zone?"

Moe was clearly taken aback by that. "Oh, not that one! I don't think it's a good idea. What do you want to do with it?"

"Remember how strange it was? It was so close to Globb's entrance, yet they ignored it."

"What are you getting at?" Moe asked.

"Clearly, there's something we squirrels don't know," Aly said. "I don't know why I keep being drawn to that place, but I can feel there's just something special about it."

Though he wasn't able to explain it, he knew what he was feeling wasn't a mere guess. Rather, it was an intuition he had developed over years of experience being a nut miner. He continued, "We need to go back to that zone, collect a lot of data and analyze them. In fact, for the coming Monday to Wednesday, we'll collect data around the clock. Don't leave any gaps."

"After that, what do we do?" Moe asked.

"By then, we'll be ready to meet the other clans."

Aly's notes

Having the courage to create and act on your point of view brings you closer to unlocking insights from the data.

Chapter 9

Storytell

BEING SUCH A dominant figure, there was no surprise that the meeting between the clan leaders was going to happen at Maq's place. The surprising part was that this meeting was actually happening. Seldom did all the four leaders meet together. Nab of Globb, Ren of Grint, and Maq weren't exactly known to be eager in settling matters at the negotiating table. They would rather fight and muscle their way through to get what they wanted. But somehow, Aly had managed to coax them into meeting this time.

He had promised them that he was bringing to the table a proposition they had never seen before and nothing like they could ever imagine. It was something that would totally change how the miners worked and even how the squirrels lived.

Aly, coming with Moe, walked into the meeting feeling confident that what they were going to show would be too good to ignore. They had spent the past week planning meticulously for this day and had everything prepared to a tee. After all, they had no choice. If they failed today, their clan wouldn't survive for much longer.

I'm ready, Aly thought. In that split moment, he felt like he was on the brink of a breakthrough. Knowing he had a solid plan and a clear reason to succeed, inferiority and doubt melted away. He didn't care whom he was talking to and what kind of response he would receive. All he cared about was to offer a better life not just for his clan but for all the squirrels in Nutancia. He was now getting to the top of his game. He felt unstoppable.

"This had better be good. I don't have a lot of time," Maq said. "Tell us what you have and what's so great about it, or we'll end this meeting in no time."

Aly cleared his throat. *This is it.* "Let me first ask, what do you all think about this whole mining business?"

"I'm no different from any of you," Nab said. Nab didn't have the frame of Maq, but his raucous voice made his presence known. "We all know how taxing it is to the miners. The maze is becoming tougher all the time. You can't really tell anymore from where the nuts will come out. I've had to bring in more miners, but it's not like we had a choice."

Ren, who had been quiet so far, raised her voice. An equally fierce personality, she didn't look happy hearing what Nab had just said. "It wouldn't be that difficult for us if you weren't so greedy and mined more than you needed!"

The conversation turned into a heated argument in a blink of an eye. "Look who's talking!" Nab said, getting defensive. "As if you're any different. I'm acting in the interest of my clan. It's my duty to plan ahead and save for the coming seasons."

"But you would still find new nuts the next time, yet you keep on building your pile," Aly made his point. "What happens to the old ones? They go bad and you have to throw them away." He didn't want to be provocative, but he couldn't stop his own temper from flaring. *Calm down, Aly. Let's keep to the plan.*

"Aly," Maq said, giving a fierce scowl. "Let's get straight to the point before I throw you out of the room. What are you getting at?"

"I'm here to propose something we've never considered before."

"Straight to the point, will you? What is it?" Maq asked.

"All the clans working together as a single nut mining team."

A brief moment of stunned silence was followed by a huge burst of laughter from the three other leaders. "Aly, that's the funniest thing I've heard all week. If you came here to entertain us, then you've succeeded," Maq said with a condescending tone.

"I promise you, if we do this, all squirrels will have more than enough to eat," Aly said. He wasn't going to be swayed from his goal. "And here's the best part. We won't have to force so many of our squirrels to go into the maze anymore. Why are we competing and spending so much time in the maze when we can work together?"

Nab rolled his eyes. "Go on. Just let me know when you're done. Since we're already here, we might as well let you finish your fairy tale."

Aly knew they weren't buying into this. *I must continue nonetheless.* "Imagine how much better life would be for the miners if they could do more fulfilling work and spend more time with their families. Imagine how much it would mean to your clan if life weren't all about pushing hard to get more and more nuts. We've become so fixated with mining nuts that we've forgotten that there's more to life than that."

"Aly, let's cut all of the nonsense now and stop pretending," Maq said. "We all know what you and your miners have been up to. There's something you know that we don't, that's for sure. If you came here thinking you could take advantage of us with that knowledge, then don't tell me you haven't been warned. I won't hesitate to go to war."

"That knowledge is precisely what I wanted to tell you about," Aly said. "Believe me. We can get more than enough nuts for all the squirrels with less than half the number of miners we have today!"

"Hey!" Ren burst into a rage. "Are you trying to take us for a ride? If you think you can come here and make fools out of us, you're choosing the wrong squirrels!"

"I know how you're feeling. But if you let me explain, you'll understand. It's definitely possible if we use data science," Aly said.

"Data science?!" Nab stood up and stared at Aly in the eyes. "Is this part of your plan to confuse and trick us into agreeing to something in your favor? It better not be, or I'll make sure your clan will never touch a single peanut ever again!"

"Nab, let him continue. We'll listen," Maq said to Aly's surprise.

Why is Maq suddenly turning soft? Does he know about data science?

Aly, boosted by Maq's change of stance, said, "Now, if you can all just take a deep breath, relax, and, just for a few minutes, take in what I have to say…"

He took out a sheet of paper showing the map of the maze. "We've been thoroughly observing this area and recorded what we saw."

Area observed

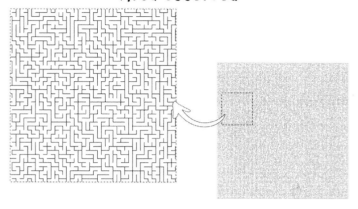

He then took out a larger sheet of paper, showing the heatmap of the nuts in that area.

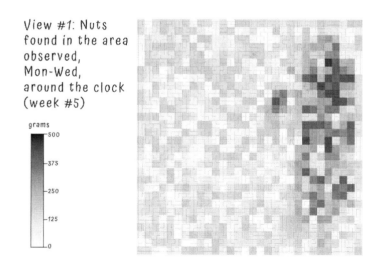

View #1: Nuts found in the area observed, Mon-Wed, around the clock (week #5)

"I'm sure you all know this area well, especially you, Nab, as it's just adjacent to your clan's entrance," Aly said.

"That's nothing new, Aly," Nab said. "Not many areas are predictable these days, but this one is. Are you telling me that most of the nuts were on the east side? My miners knew it already."

"But perhaps you haven't seen these," Aly said, as he showed another heatmap of the same exact place, but with different results.

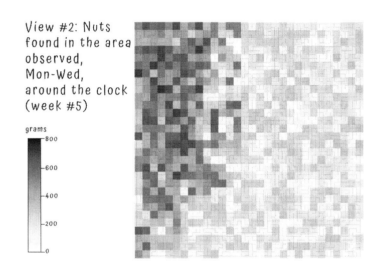

View #2: Nuts found in the area observed, Mon-Wed, around the clock (week #5)

Nab eyes bulged, looking at the paper. "Hang on, what's this showing? Why is it different from the first one? Are you saying that there were also plenty of nuts on the west side? No way!"

"Indeed, there were. This happened just last week," Aly said.

"But which of these maps is the truth?" Ren

asked, rapidly switching her view between both maps. "Both cannot be right at the same time."

"Both of them are," Aly said. "See, this is what happened. When we observed this area, we realized that the nuts would come out in two completely different ways."

Aly knew he had now managed to capture their attention. *Time to win it.* "The first map is showing something we all know well. Those are the nuts that will stay on the ground until one of us finds them and picks them up."

Aly's face beamed with delight as the other leaders inched closer and leaned toward him. "But the second map has uncovered something we've never realized before, because we were too obsessed with getting to the nuts as fast as we could."

"And what's that?" Maq asked, getting anxious.

"We realized that there were ephemeral nuts!"

Maq, Nab, and Ren looked stunned. There wasn't a single word uttered.

"They would emerge for a short while, and less than twenty seconds later, they would go back into the ground," he continued.

Aly could see bewilderment in their eyes. "Throughout the day, at the same location, these nuts could have appeared a few times. Probably more than that. But then, since they disappeared almost as quickly as they came, what would the miners see?"

"Nothing," Nab obliged.

"See, Nab," Aly said, "our miners may have occasionally been lucky if their timing had been right. But, most of the time, they would have seen absolutely nothing. Soon enough, they would leave to look for better places. But if they could have just waited—"

"Now, since they would appear a few times a day, it means there should be more ephemeral nuts compared to the permanent ones!" Ren said.

"Exactly!" Aly said. "But we still had to look at the data to confirm, and this was what it showed."

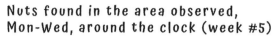

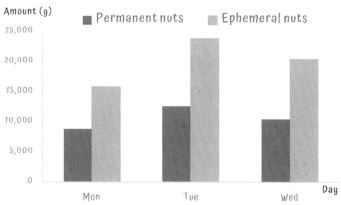

Nuts found in the area observed, Mon-Wed, around the clock (week #5)

"To be sure, we looked at a couple of other areas, and they were no different. There was almost twice as much of the ephemeral nuts than the permanent ones," Aly said.

"That's just incredible," Ren said. "We've always been proud of having the fastest and strongest miners. We've been too impatient and quickly wanted to move on to the next area, and that meant deserting these goldmines. If we could have just paused and observed..."

"Imagine if we could change our ways and work together," Aly said. "If we could strategically get our miners positioned at the right locations and mine as the nuts appear, we could collect more than enough to feed our squirrels."

"But that's easier said than done," Nab said. "How can you tell where these 'right' locations are? Yes, in some places, we can make good guesses. But the reality is, in most others, they're just random. You know that."

"I had the same question when our friend here, Moe, showed me the answer. Trust me, with data science, there's a way," Aly replied.

"Aly," Maq said. "The only way to detect these ephemeral nuts is to collect the data all the time. You didn't station your miners there with the nut scanners all day long, did you?"

Now that's strange. How does he know they're called nut scanners? "No," Aly said. "We simply installed the scanners. You wouldn't have noticed these devices if you didn't look up, but they've been continuously scanning for nuts within the area and recording the data. That's how we got these heatmaps and charts."

Aly knew his next point was going to be crucial. "But for us to continue this work, we need to work together. That's my request to all of you. No one clan could do it alone, even if I gave you the technology."

"What do you want us to do?" Nab asked.

The perfect question at the perfect time!

"To do the same thing for the whole maze," Aly said. "If, together, we could build enough of these scanners and move them around, we would have a vast amount of data to guide our mining decisions."

"Are you sure we can handle this?" Ren asked. "That sounds like a huge amount of data."

"We can," Aly said. "And that's why we need to build more computers, which is the machine to process all this data. Because we're now talking about the entire maze, it won't be the normal kind of data anymore, but *big data.*" He turned back and saw Moe smiling and giving a thumbs up.

"What is that?" Ren asked.

"Big data is different from normal data in a few different ways," Aly began. "First, because now we're talking about data continuously coming from all the scanners all over the maze, it will come at such an incredible *velocity.* Secondly, with potentially hundreds of thousands of data points coming every minute, the *volume* is humongous. Finally, once we start to record more types of data, which we can, there will be more *variety* and *veracity* in the data that we need to handle."

Aly continued. "For these reasons, we'll need to treat it differently from normal data. We'll need to have enough computers, distribute their tasks, and coordinate their work in a certain way."

"You know what? I don't need any more convincing. I'm in," Ren said.

"Me too!" Nab added.

"Aly, first let me apologize," Maq said. "I saw something was brewing within your clan, and I hated seeing it. That's when I persuaded Lex to go behind your back and give me all the knowledge I needed. I wanted to have the same, if not better, as what you had."

Aly was seething. "Lex?! No wonder!" he raised his voice.

"But please forgive him too," Maq said. "It's now time to change, and I'll be the first one to correct my ways. I know I haven't been fair to all of you, but that's now in the past. Let's work together."

"He won't get away with it," Aly said. "He needs to learn his lesson. He won't be the head of Gliff's mining team anymore, that's for sure."

Maq bowed his head in shame. "And I'll own up to my wrongdoings too. I'll step down as the head of Groar and hand it over to my general. Aly, there's no one more deserving than you to lead all of us into this new life."

Moe, who had been quietly listening throughout, leaned toward Aly and whispered, "You never gave me the chance to explain the fifth and last step of our plan, but I guess you have it in you already. It's conveying what we've learned from the data to inspire an action, called *data storytelling*. In fact, I don't think anyone else in Nutancia could've done a better job than what you did!"

Aly's face lit up in a big grin. He felt a deep sense of gratitude to have come such a long way since that fateful meeting with Moe. If the history of Nutancia would ever be written, he knew this moment would be prominently etched as a milestone. He knew this country would never be the same again.

Aly's notes

Data science has the power to unite clans and change their lives.

Epilogue

AS THEY WERE sitting at Nutancia's new nut mining operations center, Aly said to Moe, "Hey, I've always wanted to ask this. It's been bubbling in my mind for so long and I can't hold it in anymore. Tell me, how did you become such a genius and come up with so many ideas and innovations?"

"Here's the secret," Moe said. "I didn't come up with those myself. I was just using what others have discovered and adapted them to what I wanted to achieve."

"You haven't answered my question!"

"Okay, I went to the human country and learned from them!"

Aly jumped out of his seat. "What?! You actually did that? How are you still here in one piece? How did you survive going to that place?

Not after all these horror stories about humans hunting us and turning us into their food."

"With all due respect, our ancestors probably had a good reason to tell us that. But I decided not to believe that, and I went anyway. It turned out it was, indeed, not true."

"Moe, you're really crazy."

Moe burst into laughter. "That's what most squirrels would think. I was just questioning why things are how they are and if any good would come if we changed them. You don't have to be a crazy squirrel to do that, do you?"

"So, the humans already have all this technology?" Aly asked.

"Yes, I simply took what's working for them and built on it. Not hard, is it?" Moe grinned. "And since you asked, I think it's time we go even further."

"Not again!"

"Listen," Moe said. "We can advance our country, and more importantly our squirrels, in a much bigger way. It's time we started challenging ourselves and dreamed about something we've never thought of before."

Here we go again. "We're not getting ourselves

into trouble, are we?" Aly asked.

Moe went on to probe Aly even further. "Imagine how life would be if each country could benefit the other? What if we had things that humans would dearly like to have, and vice versa?"

"What are you trying to get at?"

"We should start trading with humans," Moe said, his eyes glistened.

Aly was startled. "Are you out of your mind?!"

"Calm down. I know what I'm talking about," Moe said. "I've realized that some of the resources we have in abundance are scarce in the human country."

"Such as?" Aly asked.

Moe's eyes were wide and glowing. "What else, nuts! Since we now have more than enough to eat, why don't we trade the surplus with humans? Guess what? They really love nuts."

"They do?"

"And, surprise, surprise, we can make use of data too," Moe said. "Humans' most important business decisions are made based on data."

"Really?"

Moe pulled in a deep breath. "Let me give one example. Tell me, apart from nuts, what are the other things that we can find in the maze?"

"Quite a few, like mushrooms, cocoa beans, and flowers," Aly said. "But those aren't food squirrels can eat."

"But what if humans can eat them or, better still, love them? I know of one they really love."

Aly scratched his head. "Which is?"

"Cocoa beans," Moe said. "We can turn cocoa beans into chocolates. I can't tell you enough how crazy humans are about chocolates," Moe said.

"The best is yet to come," he continued. "Humans love mixing their chocolate with other food. Guess which food is at the top of the pile? Nuts!"

Aly stood up and flung his arms wide. "Oh, and since we have nuts and cocoa beans in abundance, we can make nutty chocolate bars and trade them with humans. How amazing! But...when does the data part come?"

"Here's one example," Moe said. "Since we have different kinds of nuts, we will be selling a large variety of nutty chocolate bars. But how do we know, at a particular time, how much each of these varieties could potentially sell?"

Aly couldn't stop from pacing around the

room they were in. Moe's enthusiasm for this outrageous endeavor had now rubbed off on him. "By understanding the relationship between different features and sales from previous data?"

"Exactly! That's regression, isn't it?" Moe said. "But we can go further. A hazelnut chocolate bar may be the best-selling bar in the human country, but it doesn't mean that it's the favorite of every single person."

"So, we can predict for each person, what is his or her favorite type of chocolate bar?" Aly asked.

"Yes," Moe said. "We do this by analyzing the data of past purchases, age, gender, general interests, and other food purchased."

"Classification!"

"Spot on," Moe said. "We can use this information, for example, to personalize the buying experience, plan the types of chocolate bars to produce, and, of course, selectively mine for the most in-demand nuts. I guess collecting the data about the types of nuts won't be a waste of time after all!"

"Oh! The possibilities are just endless."

"I think you get the idea," Moe said. "But

that's just the beginning."

Aly rubbed his paws together. "Go on then."

Moe winked. "That's for another data science project!"

About the Author

Meor Amer's mission is to help create data-driven professionals and youths via an enjoyable learning experience. He has previously worked with clients in over fifteen countries for deploying telecommunications data analytics solutions and running training & enablement programs. For his MSc, he worked on machine learning techniques in biomedical engineering.

You may reach Meor at contact@edsquarelabs.com.

Visit www.edsquarelabs.com for more.

Thanks for reading! Please add a review on Amazon and let me know what you thought.

I really appreciate your feedback, and I love hearing what you have to say.

I need your input to make the next version of this book and my future books better.

Please leave me a helpful review on Amazon letting me know what you thought of the book.

Thank you
Meor Amer

Printed in Great Britain
by Amazon